What if Vietnam Never Happened? Foresight and Hindsight in Graham Greene's *The Quiet American*

Bryan W. Brickner

Ew Publishing

What If Vietnam Never Happened? Foresight and Hindsight in Graham Greene's *The Quiet American*

A phenomena pamphlet

Bryan W. Brickner

Ew Publishing

Table of Contents

Question phenomena

*For Ares, Artemis
and Daniel E. Bryan*

Question phenomena

What if in 1960 We the People had had Constitutional representation?

What if one of those Representatives had read Graham Greene's *The Quiet American*?

What if Vietnam never happened?

Bryan W. Brickner
Vandalia MI
11 November 2016

I. Foresight

Phenomenon one: CIA

'What is he? O.S.S?'

'The initial letters are not very important. I think now they are different.'

Graham Greene is writing of American involvement in Vietnam in the early 1950s, before the social upheaval of the 60s. The "initial letters" (CIA) are not the focus of this pamphlet; it is only noted that in 1955 a successful British author published a work showing the American seeding of the war known as Vietnam.

The old saying, "takes one to know one" comes to mind; Greene was a spy as well, recruited into MI6 by his sister: he worked for the British during WWII.

Phenomenon two: Colonialism

'It was Pyle again,' I said.

'Yes.'

'It was a terrible thing to do.'

'General Thế is not a very controlled character.'

There are only a few main players in Greene's book. The American is Pyle, the one working for the CIA with a cover of medical assistance.

Greene is the "I" narrator of the book, written into the character Fowler: English opium smoker, wise from hard knocks, aged.

The person quoted above saying "Yes" is Heng, a Saigon underground civilian communist that provides information to Greene's character.

General Thế was a real person, a nationalist that CIA Pyle supported, who was assassinated in 1955.

The Quiet American shows how the end of WWII marked the beginning of the US war in Vietnam: basically, the British, French, and Americans didn't think the people of Vietnam could govern themselves. It was racial and sounds absurd today; perhaps a constitutionally represented We the People in 1960 would have thought so too.

Phenomenon three: The 1954 Geneva Accords

'And bombs aren't for boys from Boston. Who is Pyle's chief, Heng?'

'I have the impression that Mr Pyle is very much his own master.'

Greene's Fowler is upset with Pyle's bookish naiveté; the "boys from Boston" reference is about Harvard and a man named "York Harding" (more on him later). When Heng is asked who controls Pyle? – The answer is no one.

The 1954 Geneva Accords ended the second French colonial period in Indo-China and recognized three countries: Cambodia, Laos and Vietnam. The agreement called for elections to be held in Vietnam to establish leadership: these never happened. In its place, the US, even though we weren't a part of the agreement, sided with Ngo Dinh Diem and his declaration of a new state, South Vietnam, in 1955.

Greene's book doesn't mention any thing about the accords and instead focuses on the French decline and the US incline.

Greene's credentials and abilities were remarkable even then, as he was hailed as the greatest English writer of his times. The US took notice and made a movie out of his story, in 1958, except their Quiet American turned everything around to the point where the American was the good guy. This happened three years (less than 36 months) after Greene's book was published. He had, obviously, hit a nerve.

Phenomenon four: Communism

At first, after WWII, it was French colonial Vietnam (Indo-China) that we supported. This was the US's early phase of involvement and it ended with the 1954 Geneva Accords. The agreement divided Vietnam into north and south at the 17th parallel, or communist and not communist. That's when we really started getting involved, which was after Greene's book of warning.

At one point in the story the political nature of it all is made clear; Greene has CIA Pyle say,

"They don't want Communism" and "If Indo-China goes ..."

We've heard that often enough haven't we? Greene was saying it while we still had time to listen:

'They want enough rice. They don't want to be shot at. They want one day to be much the same as another. They don't want our white skins around telling them what they want.'

Phenomenon five: Michigan State University

The Michigan State University Vietnam Advisory Group (MSUVAG) wrote South Vietnam's Constitution; they also did it without the founding trademark of the US Republic: an enumeration (census).

Here we have the CIA and MSU working on a fundamental political document (a constitution) that was not modeled on our own founding, but one designed for a strong leader (dictator).

The MSUVAG was hatched by the CIA to support Ngo Dinh Diem, our man in Saigon. Diem was supported by the US and nation-building money flowed through MSU. The expertise and funds began in 1955 and ran until 1962; Diem was assassinated in '63, three weeks before JFK.

There is irony and confusion here that needs clarification, and it shows us something as well. Diem declared the Republic of Vietnam in 1955 after winning a rigged election; this republic was not like the US Republic, one based on representing We the People according to numbers. In fact, Diem was a Catholic leading a Buddhist nation, and groups within Vietnam, like the Caodaists and Degar (Montagnards), were left to fend for themselves between Diem and the Vietminh.

Greene's work doesn't show the US advocating for a South Vietnam republic that counts the people and divides by a number in order to form representation, like the US Constitution mandates. Nationalism with a strong leader is what the US created in 1955 South Vietnam, not a unifying We the People concept.

Phenomenon six: General Thế

Race was an issue in replacing the French power structure that was defeated in 1954. Part of the storyline in Greene's book is the American effort to find (create) someone to support. Pyle finds General Trinh Minh Thế, a former Caodaist officer who had broken away and formed his own small band (2,000 soldiers). Thế was the real life person in Greene's novel that we (via the CIA) supported before Diem.

Here is Greene's Fowler talking of what We the People were getting into, all published in Britain in 1955 and in the US in '56:

How often I had explained all this before. I was a record always turned on for the benefit of newcomers – the visiting Member of Parliament, the new British Minister. Sometimes I would wake up in the night saying, 'Take the case of the Caodaists.' Or the Hoa-Hoa or the Binh Xuyen, all the private armies who sold their services for money or revenge. Strangers found them picturesque, but there is nothing picturesque in treachery and distrust.

'And now,' I said, 'there's General Thế. He was Caodaist Chief of Staff, but he's taken to the hills to fight both sides, the French, the Communists ...'

Then American Pyle interjects, saying what *'the East needed was a Third Force.'*

Phenomenon seven: US Congress

Recall that Greene was MI6; the 1958 US-made distorted version of his *The Quiet American* points to something else as well: Greene knew what he was talking about and the US government knew he knew.

Greene writes of a visit to Saigon from the US Congress. This prompts a discussion of the Third Force, or national democracy, which isn't a US-like We the People republic. Dominguez is speaking here, Greene/Fowler's assistant who works the Saigon underground:

'Then someone asked him [Pyle] some stock question about the chances of the Government here ever beating the Vietminh and he said a Third Force could do it. There was always a Third Force to be found free from Communism and the taint of colonialism – national democracy he called it; you only had to find a

leader and keep him safe from the old colonial powers.'

'It's all in York Harding,' I said. 'He had read it before he came out here. He talked about it his first week and he's learned nothing.'

'He may have found his leader.'

II. Hindsight

Phenomenon one: York Harding

'York Harding might write in graphic abstractions about the Third Force, but this was what it came down to – this was It. There was a door in the back wall; it was locked, but the key was on the desk among the pencils. I opened the door and went through.'

"York Harding" poetically shadows Greene's book; it's a nonce name that, like all names, is meant to convey something. This one obviously means Yale and Harvard because of the CIA connection; but there's more, as that's too simple for Greene: Harding is a clue, and so is York.

President Harding died under peculiar circumstances in 1923 and was succeeded by Calvin Coolidge. Harding was a We the People kind of president and had enemies.

York is a famous city in England with a white rose as its emblem. *The White Rose* was also the name used by Munich pamphleteers in Nazi Germany. They were active from June 1942 to February 1943, at which time they were caught. Three were sentenced to death for treason and guillotined the same day; one of them, Hans Scholl, cried out before the blade fell: *"Es lebe die Freiheit!" "Long live Freedom!"*

Phenomenon two: Poets

Greene prefaces his story with two quotes from British poets: one from A. H. Clough and the other from Byron. With Clough we are reminded of "our terrible notions of duty" and through Byron the folly of good intentions.

The quotes from Clough and Byron highlight a counter-dialogue running through *The Quiet American*. It might be only noted because of perspective: we now know Greene was MI6 and describing the CIA. The way Vietnam happened in the 50s and not the 60s, via the CIA supporting a colonial power against non-whites, rings hollow today. There should be an echo, a resounding noise, some Nazis or people to hate. There isn't. In Greene's analysis, the hate is coming from US policy; the tragedy was unfolded upon and spread by the US, and yet the drama was written (in blood) mostly by and for others. Greene saw that the 20th century was playing as Byron had said of the 19th: '*This is the patent age of new inventions for killing bodies, and for saving souls, all propagated with the best intentions.*'

Phenomenon three: The 1958 Quiet American

The 1958 movie version of *The Quiet American* was also set in Saigon starting in '52. Greene notes the year in his book as well; he closes the work of "fiction" with real dates: March 1952 – June 1955. This places our initial involvement CIA-wise to the early 1950s, during the Truman administration.

Greene called the '58 movie version of his book a "propaganda film for America." It starred Medal of Honor recipient Audie Murphy as Pyle and whitewashed the main Vietnamese female character (Phuong) with an Italian. Moreover, the '58 version made the Americans out to be the good guys, totally flipping Greene's insights. Edward Lansdale was the CIA agent in Vietnam (the man Greene used to build Pyle) and he helped with the flipping: Lansdale worked, un-credited, on the 1958 rewrite. They must have been some good edits, as Murphy felt it was one of the greatest roles he ever played.

Dwight Eisenhower was president from 1953-61, so he laid the Vietnam foundation with military aid and Michigan State sponsoring Diem; JFK inherited this by squeaking out a victory in 1960 over Vice President Nixon.

Phenomenon four: JFK

The Vietnam CIA operative Lansdale was Greene's Pyle; Greene modeled his character on Lansdale's work and the bombing material (plastics) provided to the very real General Thế.

JFK is handed our Vietnam policy in January 1961; the new president is inaugurated on the 20th and meets with Lansdale (Pyle) on the 28th. Lansdale had just visited South Vietnam and brought shocking news: the communists had infiltrated South Vietnam and it was hardly safe anywhere.

Kennedy was impressed with Lansdale-Pyle's knowledge and wanted to name him ambassador to South Vietnam. The State Department and CIA said no; by 1961 they had had enough of Lansdale-Pyle and said he wasn't a "team player."

Phenomenon five: Opium

On 23 March 1961, two months into his presidency, JFK gave a news conference on Laos and Vietnam. There was a map showing Laos, North Vietnam and some of "Communist" China; the map had an area shaded black that was in North Vietnam and bordered the other two: Lai Chau, part of the Golden Triangle.

Fowler, Greene's British war correspondent, is an opium smoker throughout the book. He usually smokes in the evening, and at the beginning of the book, as the police are questioning him about Pyle's death, he is on opium and writes of what that is like. Later in the book Fowler "visits" (from the air) the Golden Triangle while on a French bombing mission.

Vietnam offered questions of being and becoming; for the American Pyle, it was about subjects and objects and truths: being.

For the British Fowler, it was about transformations; first from French colonialism to Japanese occupation, back to French colonialism and then, seemingly, to communism or America's Third Force: becoming.

Neither is or would have been clearly correct; understanding the co-dependence of both was entirely clear and correct.

Phenomenon six: Censorship

The effect of censorship runs throughout Greene's book; the French are always reading and editing what he sends out of the country (to London) via cable.

The accepted French narrative is that communists are doing the evil; Greene's Fowler knows it is General Thế via support from the CIA. Greene can't write that though and make it news, so he writes and publishes *The Quiet American.*

Greene's book was published a year after the Geneva Accords were signed, and the same year General Thế was killed (assassinated in Saigon on 3 May 1955).

Phenomenon seven: PFC Bryan

Daniel E. Bryan was eight-years old in 1955, not that I knew him; I wasn't born yet myself. I found his name listed with the other soldiers killed from Illinois at the Vietnam War memorial in downtown Chicago. He was just a name among many that caught my eye, so I looked him up.

PFC Bryan had only been in Saigon (Gia Dinh) for about a month when the Tet Offensive began on 30 January 1968. Bryan was in the infantry and a member of a unit with lineage to the US Civil War, the 18th Infantry Regiment: he died from small arms fire on 8 February 1968.

Daniel E. Bryan
27 OCT 1947 – 8 FEB 1968

What if We the People ...